Deifying A Total Darkness

many villages were razed for this. most were internal.

thanks to my various fams, real, imagined, or cobbled together:

rother & helen, karen, deborah, & jackie, dorsie jean, journey & jordan, delainia & elainia, gerald & isaac. the poets at once upon a time in the projects, the international house of poets, teneice durrant, joseph rathgeber, and the clubhouse gang (jude mcpherson & tina andry - *we proly finna go to hell anyway*).

for

Crystal & Zaria

Deifying A Total Darkness

upfromsumdirt

Harry Tankoos Books

CONTENTS

popular poem w/ sharp title 3

the houngan's space capsule 4

here, the earth giant lays his gentle head 5

jean rabin gives africa the bird 6

the parabola of the sower 8

the witch's titty has a cold nipple (*& still i choose to suckle*) blues 9

meth lab at the lollipop guild 11

poem for a broken brazier 14

just put your lips together and blow 15

photographer catches the exact moment a volcano erupts 16

black begonias 18

caul & response 20

1369 22

the philosopher with the bantu overbite 24

bus fare for a valkyrie 25

abstrack africana no. 1 27

in deifying a total darkness 28

short poem for a black love theme 32

anansi with the laughing face 33

crissy, from the creek 35

after the electro-magnetic pulse has failed to kill us 38

black poet persona poem 40

bang 42
kizzy declares to a custom agent 44
help me get the body in the trunk 45
extra celestials 48
orisha obsidious 50
bysshe, please 52
modern xenopmorph 58
to have the wish i wish tonight 60
here, the earth giant dreams himself a cloud 64
pell grant for a space force 65
dirt farmer 68
cul-de-sac safari 69
psalm for an underexcavated hum 80
abstrack africana no. 15 81
upfromsumdirt applies for a job 82
engine block feng shui for boy davis' only son 84
a small poem to let you know the end is near 87
a time unraveller's travel journal 89
a time unraveller's travel journal: the sankofa paradox 102
protoplasmic phrenology 107

why should we the sons of the land
plead unheeded before your shrine,
when our hearts are full of song
and our lips trembling with sadness?

- Kwesi Brew

maybe i'm mad,
for the voices are luring me,
urging me from the midnight
moon and the silence of my desk
to walk on wave crests across a sea

- Gabriel Okara

your hand is heavy, Night, upon my brow,
i bear no heart mercuric like the clouds, to
dare exacerbation from your subtle plough.

- Wole Soyinka

dot dot dit dit dot dot dash

- Gil Scott-Heron

Deifying A Total Darkness

Popular Poem w/ Sharp Title

i've written a wicked thing
a bane a pox upon you
if i name it *poem* you'll read it
with tender teeth you'll read it
with pillows in your breath

"bated"

you'll see the word poem
and expect a delicate dialogue
as pedestal for the pristine the precious
even if it beheads your father
its vehicular verse running down your mother
stealing everything you own you'll look at
all the blood
with your tongue dabbing like a cotton swab
but you will not listen to its lungs
in heavy labor congested and heaving
and calling you names to your face
its sole existence: to ply you with expletives
cursing, as if noah, your children, your clan
your valley of wet bones my prescription
~~peace of mind~~ for world peace
"this *poem*"
you'll say
"has given me life!"
you'll say it sets the pace.
& you'll share it like a plague.

The Houngan's Space Capsule

the space suit explodes petals cascading
black with purple tips a roiling heat since
liftoff / the astronaut was a houseplant
ev'ry petal a ghanian metal
then gold medallion and then a labret
for the bottom lips of nonwhite poets
drifting throughout their diasporas // each
stem a song however it's said in space
no one can hear you theme / the metaphor
denied metaphrase unless of course they
now you not unless of course they *here* you
once they here you they have you gifting you
their vainglory for alight speeds // stardust
collapses into your standard chorus:
the soft pale torso of james t kirk and
his angled jaw in opposing orbits
around mournfully distant suns and the
observatory (lonely) warps away
the black astronaut left straining at stars
left to decipher oxygen levels
the uncharted ode / soft allegories
useless for wander or habitation
this oversampled earth unfit to map
explore habitat populate / so we
terraform home landscapes made alien.

Here, The Earth Giant Lays His Gentle Head

the goal / to be more than a translator of mud
for you: not for you / this phantasm as poem / the poem
as permutation / my head under the guillotine
of too many syllables until decapitation / my disquisition
without restraint or quarantine // the goal / to be immortal
until i am good and dead / the golden made pure until obsidian
the enshrinement of tongue until all song is emancipated

please stop with your praise for inertia

i will no longer enshrine paralysis with you / my lips
are not lazy / i'm just disinclined movement by your sermon
the sleek automaton of your stanzas worshipping the oscitant

what a fool you taught of me gilding cherished marble
with spit and spirit that whittles preferred light
from precious night exchanging birthright & dowry
for academic exposition my vernaculars annotated / my footprint
turned a footnote   the asterisk-american

my goal: to not be you / my goal is to live forever beyond
for aeons & atoms & anatomy to age out / for even in night
i cast a shadow your entire body would have to dilate to see.

Jean Rabin Gives Africa The Bird

Darwin would be amazed how in your very hands dragons dissolve
into hummingbirds, dinosaurs into starlings. you made the science

of subterfuge a primary tenet of art history; painting cardinals
and the occasional pigeon in watercolors and the white-wash

of racial vertigo. but in which sketchbook are your vultures hidden?
oh forgive me this inquisition, the great John Audubon has every

right to give Africa *the bird* this bantam red with peacock's plume
chest puffy behind the ruffled poet's silken shirt

it's written that Charles Darwin never gave credence to mayhem
or mystics but surely he favored the magician's slighting hand

Dear Jean, your tale's an epitome *survival of the fittest* — 1-part
Harry Houdini, 1-part Bundini Brown; you, escape artist joie de vivre

prototype for Colonel Sanders — 11 herbs and 4 michelin stars
instilled in every sketch, pigments that literally drew you away

from your origins, every thin line escaping Haiti and the money-
brokers set to deny you inheritance; a favored son adopted

by Kentucky and France, you do so love being everything
but what you are: the illegitimate love-child of a chambermaid

and her plantation-owning pirate - not that i'm judging! who would choose sugarcane over Eiffel Towers? you're not the first

nor the last to sugarcoat a nativity scene. but still you do love
New Orleans, claiming the Queen's City as your place of birth

the only place on God's Green Earth where you found (under the
auspices of debauchery) revelry for your darker strokes. but Bacchus

was never a patron saint of Haiti. Baron Samedi is your crown.
Brother Eshu Elegbara guards your gates and escape routes.

maybe there's more Dahomey owning you than you'd ever admit
to knowing as sankofa too is a bird — you could be the Bennu

of the Bluegrass! in Africa concentric circles also have their own
secret societies; you, Mr. Frontier-Ornithologist, would fit right in

as there's a role for scarecrows in all the various artforms of
Santeria. you see you've misconstrued the venerable beliefs

of your father's favorite lover to be the vulgarities of your father's
wife - again not a judgment - but Darwin also believed in dodos

and if not in the phoenix then most certainly in its metaphor: in
the egg of your soul, John, Jeanne Rabin too takes flight; draw that.

The Parabola Of The Sower

the "black problem"
is only our refusal to predate you
making black narcissism canon

how empty of me i am walking in your shoes
this watermelon tasting like your tongue
you lose my son and i cry out for him in your language

crying in facebook
never laughing in swahili

i wore an armani suit
to my day of judgment waiting in line
to meet st. peter and when i finally got to God
asking if She'd seen my son She gasped

Her fraying blouse revealing sun she said
Mungu Wangu, Unaonekana Huzuni!

my face to chest Her breasts caught my tears
She cried *Nani Anayethubutu Kukuumiza Hivi?*

my spirit wept in the compost
praying for translation.

The Witch's Titty Has A Cold Nipple (& Still I Choose To Suckle) Blues

ornithology filled the moon
on the night that i was born
said Charlie Parker was my God
on the night Mama spat me out
- i'm an innercity
auspex reading half-eaten
chicken wings in the gutters of a curb.
        said: i was an astrological concierge
        catchin' trains and jumpin tracks
        where a Nigga's soul is dark alluvium
        at the bottom of his words
i was raised on Witch's Titty
and i suckled all the sauces, swallowed
African Sorcery's every ounce
        said: i said some fancy magic shit,
        skippin' stars like stones
        across your senses; reckless eyes a'rollin'
        your 2 tongues just a-click-clackin'
listen,
i was raised high on salience
lips braised (until bruised) on The Holy Breasts
of Mother Ma'at; Joseph's Mary rolled me in her womb,
until Jesus, jealous, spat into my bourbon & yelled
it's time i met my maker
        — HA!

but on death-threats i slept.
        said: my somnifacience
        oscillates like owl-shit on a shoulder-blade,
        what a beauty mark to behold
but i'm not the kind of blue
to suppress hexes out of hue
and like any Shining Black X, it isnt
something to make me lose confidence
in what i'm doing. you see,
Auset is such a songstress
her teeth crusted in diamonds and kohl,
she's been my waitress many years;
keeps her stockings full of switchblade,
has my back where i am blind.

i'm grand sommelier of all the shadows
& my Wadjet always watches.
        said: croon me and i surface;
        huff and puff and i appear.
Brother Khepra keeps all my secrets;
Albert Ayler tracks the score.

Meth Lab At The Lollipop Guild

1

scene 1: an allegory - back alley Mount Olympus:
the demigod of dayglow in dungarees & a three-quarters coat:
"psst! ...hey, slim... slim. you good? i got what you creed."

2

stuck in a screed / *"Apollo Saccharinalia:*
the Ascension of Paula Deen to a Sistine Chapel
as American literary culture" - a dissertation.

3

"no spin at the loom for the autodidactic" says
Caption America: The Winter Writer - scene 2:
(....*one motherfuckin two motherfuckin three*)

4

"it's the drummer; i've come to bleed the calf."
the blood pooling at the feats of the giant Frost, the bronze Biz,
the holy Soyinka, and the wick-wick-wack alike

5

Shakespeare sits up in his grave: *"all lines matter"*
when all are blind not even the dimmer switch is sacred
we black ocular or we bukowski better - our two towers

6

scene 3: *"i'm not a diner, not until you let me dine"*
every poem interred at the Shrine of the Black Madonna:
the blood-tick in ancient amber with infectious mastodon within

7
"Well uhh, ahh-oooh - I stretched out and yawned"
it's either Oh, Mighty Dawn, Awning Of All Effulgent Domains
or The First Time I Received Good Head It Caused An Eclipse

8
scene 1 (reshoot): Frodo Kills Boq & Becomes Munchkin King:
the former hobbit with a fascist habit has a toupee of navel oranges
his syringes are free, *"but the kraaken costs money, oh yea-uh"*

9
series reboot: we open on the moon: 2 poets sit on swings at
the astronaut graveyard streaming podcasts & feeding clay pigeons
to literary journals / faster than light - *"My God, it's full of stars!"*

10
at Jericho's Wall Rammelzee & Papa LaBas toss lots for the future
of American Lit's Full Black Lip / for a good time text submissions
as SMS to 8675309 - *"I bet you monsters lead innnnteresting lives."*

11
@TheRealDoctorZeus√ night-tweets to call Black Lit a #FakeMyth
but Night's Mouth is a tacklebox where language is a single long lure:
"syncin' up our master plans ain't nothin' but syntax inside our hands."

12
the princess sits up, 40 featherbeds aloft / *"is it the pea?"* inquires
the Queen / *"yes, but no; it's the poet with whom i bunk; he snores in*

my bouffant, my powdered wig awashed in his drool of dark poems"

13
a tree falls on a florist; birdhunters gather in a meadow
peacocks stalk the outer rim / lumberjacks cower in the dim / and
how's the old adage go? - *"pull the roots and disclaim the shovel"?*

14
scene 1: at last: the Sims: AWP / and how many poets does it take
to ekphrasis a lightbulb? a commercial break begins in 8 seconds
then we pedagogy in plain sight / *"slowly he turned, step by step"*

15
<curriculum vitae> the editor who white-professored was a black
poet / each metaphor a gold splattered plaster of zzzZeus *"But us
gon' bust you in the mouth with a Horus now"* </curriculum vitae>

16
All Of Me / the woodchipper brogue / the caesura in our eyes
boycotting deference to marble / a canon of Scott Joplin, Outkast,
Assata Shakur, & Frantz Fanon / yes, Love, *Why Not Take All Of Me?*

Poem For A Broken Brazier

this song of soot and cinder
tiny hymn for tender ash

this world a hearth exhausted
our every kiss devoid of kindle

Just Put Your Lips Together And Blow

Poetry found me in the solarium / sound asleep
it was years since i'd last poured honey in these wounds
i could never see nature softly / as told / as some
newborn in need of swaddling & a room-tempered teat
something like i recall saying:
        if the arcadian is to be tampered with then i'll steep it
        in tequila and deep-fry that bitch in animal fat.

that's all the strength i can muster for the idyllic.

so yes, *Dear Fidelity,* the love in my heart
for the outdoors is grossly varicose and cares not
for the romance of Greater Nature / forgive
the insouciance / i suspect it's inherited

                                        perspective:
Emmett Till was murdered on this date August 28th
(a cryptozoology for people of color) and it's from such
i came to neuter Human Nurture / never once
did i blame the river for His interment in deep waters
but everytime i swim i too steep and now
the mermaid (within) settles for the creeks
of little depth and is secure enough to weep
in shallow water's slender embrace where
only our allowance of fealties can whistle at the wind.

Photographer Catches The Exact Moment A Volcano Erupts

- for Freddie Gray & the City of Baltimore

it begins with tectonics and anticlines and continental
drift. a seismic shift when the contents are heated

the mantle hopes for diapirism, where passions bulge
and decompress, gradual but volatile. with slates of skin,

our plates pass and rub us raw - we consider it a terrestrial
antagonism reducing 4 (or so) centuries of push and pull

to a single day: the (re)birth of the universe in a pant
for air; the collapse of Gia's own event horizon.

some would call such a spew "spiritual," an infernal faith
channeled through space and time... a systemic science

that funnels magma carta like a broken trail
(or a ruptured spine) into bright bewildering.

a temporal sweat; the core of us coming to a head
until the opposition gives and all erupts. the flaring

of the supernal. yes, we are taught to condemn the molten,
to call it names and misappropriate its character   but, O'

how there is such a crepuscular beauty within the body
of the igneous; the bowels of Heaven divinely flaring

celestially creeping to our very doorsteps! yes, the Earth,
it heaves, inhales and sighs and only wants to breathe.

the lungs open / a fusillade of blood and life; but
after all, what poet doesn't romanticize Vesuvius?

and what if Consecration has a black body? would you
still sacrifice your blue-eyed virgins? their blonde

heads in the hands of Black Pluming Gods. would you salt
the earth? would you still pray for a bountiful harvest?

Black Begonias

petal 1.
the hypothesis for an absolute ablution: a blues
with an epsom enough aura / Flora Africanus, a new
brood indigenous to where big bang is darkest;
black whole theories in a fetal phrase / the umbilical cord
between genesis and the ghosts of Ghana; this love
is black begonias for the new egun.

petal 2.
there is black ice in the briar patch. tarbaby burns
all the ivory books - protection from a pandemic
that rebirths poetry from a playstation

tarbary has a bethel between her lips
what a dark brothel her brogue a pseudo-glottological
fossil that hymns and haws and says, "i'll save you."
our call:
        "swing low Sweet Harriet, we wanna ride"
her response:
        "come-come now, chameleon; I have room."

petal 3.
the carbon cracks / Abstrack Africana forms & flourishes
in this 21st century shell. from this ochred cocoon
the incandescent crawls out, a dark fauna well versed in vertigo
the crystallization of a real kohl kudzu creeping from asphalt
leaping into language / a new non-anger
full of unknown umbers the dark symphony for a sweetpotatopeople;

what a brutal appetite this harmony / this conversation
with umbral openings & a nappy tongue - a beautiful abyss
our new, Africa-like mythology, half Atlantis half Middle Passage

in this alabaster room I bloom tenebrously.
our shared kiss radiantly glooming.

Caul & Response

1.

ephemeral voices float to me in union,
disembodied cadences from the corners
of the used bookstore in which I work;

I wait here at the register, the cashier
for colluvial languages. for 7.25 an hour
I sell you the bind off my back; my spine spent,
tongue bent into infinity shapes & adinkra signs.
I'm a shaman whose black brogue
is a dark spectrum speaking of bantu knots
standing atop soapboxes.

2.

my anonymity is indivisible;
that's nothing but the Ile-Ife' in me,
like a gen x-george clinton-conqueroo chasing chants.
I'm member #325 of the Ky Poro Guild, a son of Eshu
in a store-clerk cloak.
I've learned that invisibility
is advantageous when there is blood in your brogue.
the liturgies etched in my canon
are decisively conclusive: Achebe and Danticat,
Soyinka, Clifton, Brooks and Reed; my inner-voice
is well-read.

I was born to have voodoo doo-wop through poetry
where culturally broken words chisel the facade

and erode the misperception that black culture,
(in order to commune with nature)
passes every movement through concrete.

in the past,
ghost-stories would engrave slave-words into skin;
but where snakes shred themselves of scales,
I've learned to shed shrapnel. in dreams, Sweet Harriet
swings low, carries me from Rome.

3.
anyway, Orishas are origami for crepuscule
with college-rule; newsprint folds into a paper crown
covering the Ori of this living orator.
language is as lawn-chair for the living dead
and southern pidjin is my grateful Egun; black poems
parade our ashes in a natural state of ashé.
like a QueenMother, Black Memory pulls a halo
from a 3rd world pelvis, so (by portent), I indulge
in a self-induced patina: the policy stamping
the null and the void on every one-sided transaction
where all sales were said final;
the merchandise from transatlantic trades relinquished,
refurbished, refinished & returned home

(or wherever.)

1369

1371
i don't know how to tell you to feel
compelled loving me; to copy & paste.
to save a positive jpeg of us to your pinterest.

          to paint a quaint spouse black;
seeing gardenias not gun powder in orbit
crowning the heads of her brown babies

ruminate, with romance, on the elegance
of her earlobes, her stretch marks, her keloids;
every poem her constant companion, her carriage

across every threshold; our mouths her entryway
to privilege and a life of promise; our songs to her
at play in beds of rosebuds and pomegranate seeds

her kitchen's common kink
cast in diamonds and pearls
on the highest of billboards.

1370
Akhenaton knew the worth of a simple narrative
monopolizing light and power before heathen scribes
misinterpreted and made his single pantheon monotheistic

1369
Whitewash Jones precursed invisibility

his harmonica a shadow of self; his immortality
a magic act / Nkrumah In The Dust:

in the left corner, the incessant
challengerrr, Luuucas Beauuuchamp.
in the corner to my right, Biggerrrr
Thomas, our infernal champeen!

twin bevels of a plymouth rock,
or so said a signifyin' chimp

Planet of the Apophonies

"but i am not a simian," said the semiotician;
"monkey seize what monkey's due" says the guerrilla.

The Philosopher With The Bantu Overbite

go and find your troubles beyond the tree line;
a hermit unto yourself. return as the Hairyman
eyes red with love & riot, a huntsman haunting.
let none tame the wool or the wild. roar & smile:
the Wolof in sheep's clothing; a sorcerer dressed
in sharkskin soot possessing seven rows of teeth
and speaking love. the virgin's femur as floss
her tender gaze the password to your fairytales.

Bus Fare For A Valkyrie

Q: where are the brazen poems
lashing apocryphal authorities with fire
in counter measures to police brutality?

the lit fuse in physical flight as metaphor
for swinging, breathing, driving, singing (*ruses and muses*)

a sun-dressed child, black and 10, handcuffed
to a carousel, quietly smiles, facedown, at a colony
of ants dismantling cookies into a cosmos of crumbs;
the armored cop above her takes a knee to her back,
taking selfies with rip roaring laughter while a volley
of spectators look on, youtube's benign, guerilla loaf.

I've known poems to vibrate like the glass plate of a CVS
but never go virile enough to checkmate white supremacy
or simile an assembly of swat teams into final submission
there are no poems burning literal hell through a kevlar vest
like snipers for a black mass in self-sentience
never has a poem been written that kills its enemy for I
have tried and failed free verse like drone strikes in service
of the disenfranchised and even when writing of pink unicorns
in utopian gardens of mint my quivers are concussed
a schizophrenic sun foams over the earth and the stars pull out their
hair screaming until hoarse into the night an apoplectic moon
hoards its fullness and never surrenders its wane to the sea
our civil suppositions were written in the shadows of a lynching
this plague of democracy a puzzle where holocaust performs

due diligence monopolizing all conjectures on race.
so how do i justify to progeny my simple trove of poems?
"*huzzah!* - discordant verse as balm for the rope burns
around your neck; this inheritance of long, jarring prose,
overworked sonnets to a disemboweled lover; this recherché
for revenge; a pâté of pegasus — *children-abandoned-by-civility:*
please come forward and have your fill"

(*muses and ruses*) how does the code-switching poet decry
existential nihilism without jeopardizing a genius grant?

A: from the skull of an angler fish,
    (etiolant from edacious hunger) the head
    of the pink unicorn dangles like bait.

Abstrack Africana No. 1

white clouds are carnivorous. alien.
never stare into a cloud when it smiles;
fork tines, too, are a silver lining. and
these leaves, constantly green and dying
at my feet / leeching onto spirit
to keep from drying out:

this fornication of flora,
me falling away from laughter;

the fungal self in dark abscission.

In Deifying A Total Darkness

there is an absence of light on the dark side of the moon
that lacks mystery once it's been googled.

for one and all it's sans beauty after the browser opens.

there is anxiety for the supremacists chomping at the bit
to turn Mars into an ashtray / a meth lab / a dining hall,
a sleight debris made from material malnutrition...

there's little entitlement for remaining dark. no praise song
for the hurricane lamp full of whale oil and its seldom used
wick of coarse, nappy hair.

i feel an extemporaneous cancer closing in; i wonder
if illness, in its wildest dream, will cite a romance
in our destruction. will malignancy beatbox in couplets?

archaic cannibalism is the most honest form of commerce;
they fed us metaphors when hunger burned ugly within.
we gorged on unlimited data to placate the starvation.

the expensive broach made of mud brick and cinder block
and placed atop a pedestal for .10¢ a touch.

the whip's lash with its gift of welt adding indecipherable
glyphs to a human ledger; each layer of skin a table of contents:

across Poor Gordon's back: *an abacus of abuse.*

a blackness denied the use of liberty as a wallet for words.

Marchen:

the steadfast templar agonized his ownership
of stolen goods: a variety of freedom papers and
property deeds, a grand theft notarized - until
he resurmised his faith's irreproachable creed
easing him into the most comfortable slumber.

The Moral:

white patriarchy is greater than a sleep number.

addiction to the pitch dark was deemed a hallucinogen
as were all of the insurrectional oeuvres romanticizing
<var> *the disavowed nigger-hooligan* </var>

the 20th century was just as doomed in its end
as it was at its start. everything but jingoism falls apart.

cowbells & headlamps, please, for all the things that bump
for the night; paracletes for the gloom-bird's hated screech...

medicinal religion is a faithless contagion, a burl deep
in the esophagus of a god unable to gargle...

this language for flowers, the ritual for a tactile sense of empty;
our contempt is a contiguous hymn.

this sacred verdict for what remains fossilized in the human
body: we are anthropologists for the anatomy of lies, arsonists
who dream ourselves the theme song for landlocked astrology.

our lust for lumens is a sacred art for there is no nasdaq for
the dark and the damp. no prize money for our sweaty sloe.

this corona of black skin: we refuse to not let our ghosts be
fancy: sally hemings, *esq.*, emmett till, *odalisque*.

when's the last day you weren't force fed enlightenment?

our formal attire fit for a sarcophagus, an abstract black
sacramentalism / a love so deeply enshrined, its viscera
is jarred until deified...

we will one day burn the galaxy to the ground, setting the
rings of saturn on fire in effigy to the halos forbidden us.

each tooth a tiny skull. our golden tongues a swollen hull
for the songs that give quarter to the divine...

someday, all of this will draw to an end; a contending beauty
for the eventide, vetting exactly what it reserves; the protagonist,

sweet & sable, dissolving into our cogent love:

as soft as it is caliginous;
its umbras cast in marble.

Short Poem For A Black Love Theme

you can't withstand the steeping:
this continual tea leaking cobalt, i know this;
but how else can i expose you to plum?

deep within the rust and the ruins of this
crusting refinery there's this unhusked coo,
a slushing unhushed wonder

Anansi With The Laughing Face

a blood-bourn jazz
blaring this nuisance of neon
ruining the sheen
of mr. clean's marble — we are
mosquitos in the ears
of Monstrous Zeus
fearing our bite
when we've only come to buzz:

self-paregoric

we've learned to praise the pathogen
leviathans in leisure with canopic jargon

your diaphanous icons & dim dandies
(cirrocumulus in nature) telling us
where to apply the baby powder
in assumptions of service / black people
with brushes of rouge
at the sole discretion
of high cheek bones with a low brow

the hymn locked: *"shoo, polish!"*
is the black poet's eternal stanza

this million mosquito arch,
this swarm song of sand & asphalt
as feral as we are floral

said to be inconsequential
with our serial slang

the "artless" with a gargoyle's yodel

nacreous words that gargle
the candescence of sun
sculpting fractals of god
from geometries of sorrow / see

it says so right here:

written in central african sanskrit
on the back of some kentucky slaver's
bill of sale - it's just

you have to hold it to the sky
in full light   against the sun
                         where all will see.

Crissy, From The Creek

around the eyes
within the darkest brown
the kindness we seek is found

after brow is unfurled
beneath existential brooding
the grains of which are heaven

i look here to you
seeking not societal abeyance
for from birth you are beautifully

abundant and that is no secret
you soft brown shell of a woman
hindered so hard in happiness

it tripwires the gold cores
in my brainpan and i too
become apt / a simple

reclamation of humanity
when told to hold on to
revolutionary designs

but i don't require
narcoleptic sibilations
on the worth of skin

i come
inquiring as to its weight - how
spirits unfold when cold fingers

curl into a new lover's palm
the chromatic skin of motor oil
with its small rejuvenations leaked

onto the fallen faded leaf
a vigor restored from deep
within its veins / the unmooring

of light from the vellums beneath
burnishings as moist as voice
irrigate the spirit

or perhaps the reverse
but i'm not bowed here
for lost fables abating linguistically

some conversational clapperclaw
hit me with the heft of the here
the fullness of right now

the autopsy from the currential
merging of our shadows / exposed
viscus is neither a pratfall

nor a catcall or a battlecry
and if i ever tell you to smile
it's only because i am trying

to save myself a mendicancy
of the immediate / marginalized
heroes rising to the supernal.

After The Electro-Magnetic Pulse Has Failed To Kill Us

if   and once we've awakened covered
in mucus dark as the end of days and slither limbless
one across another in unearthed postulation every pore
a new property and you crawl to me for requisition
or appropriation / for confiscation & seizure
our dead eyes crushed with carbon
having grown accustomed to the long dark empty
of this un-renewable world / our sloe skins
dispersing nitrogen & other atoms blackened
and airborne from a crestfallen heaven

up to our breastmeats in the remnants
of a crumbled apart moon / tonsils thrashing
in labyrinths of neon our teeth rendered soft & mute
and unable to contain the properties of speech

the phosphoral grown vascular and pulsing
and pulsing down deep within our throats
with only touch and tongue to radiate syllable

singing odes through our damp lubricious pelts
our digital prosthetics made sulfur & claw
the metallic gods starved until coital & fertile
in the wireless obedience of our humid vulgar breath
where bloodletting is the only return to light

after entirely the old prior order is a broken apart ember
our bodies (shrapnel & softspot) as valley for some
small warmth in cities of ice forged on fallen hymn
while the low hanging limbs above throb tho bereft
of fruit these barren broughs passing for sky / with every
sea set to boil where we shred skins whet with desire

a manifest devouring

after all and once and nothing else
after all and once and nothing: *everything*

if (by definition) civilization remains for us
a rapacious comfort then might we as one
reclaim clinging to such a comfort / planting ourselves
in whatever shapes remain considerate to us
in soft conjugal repast / once (in dark repose) the universe
is permanently felled may we lean still
in the unctuous shimmers that loving each other (in all wisdom)
has left behind? your kiss a sweet sac of seed & ash
to my lips / the lascivious & the insidious sweet balm
of *if*

if

a clabbered sweetness yet prevails.

Black Poet Persona Poem

1.

the blockhead atop my shoulders is all hot sauce
and soapstone, but if i show it i'm called "attraction"
not "artist"... so i'm crafty and sit all day in these
songhai stirrups[1] - melanin obfuscated into meringue
until you eat it / make you think this frank's redhot
is a ghost pepper[2] : the most-paved route
for a black poet blueprinting his way to a pulitzer
is to impregnate precious ivory with field holler
in the shape of sonnets and   ~~*presto!*~~   voilà!!
but on my mamanem / i swair to fuckin' god
i will not sing for you the prerequisite woe!
mr. bojangles was beautiful for his survival
skills / for his illusion of burnt cork over a black face.
but strategist or tom, he made a mint and still died broke.
so i will not change my tune / not for your 'likes'
or for the likes of you; this is just the fine-tuning for
our final exchange / all elegba-like / where one door closes
a worm hole opens / not unlike your corny old loki
i'm low key on a high horse coming to cross rhodes & kill
hitler / be ephemeral sunshine for the over-wrought mind[3]

2.

yes. i'm "black black" as a poet
but if i openly say as much the neo-traditionalists
lose they collective goddamn shit[4] masking
their insufferable shudder with misappropriating praise

3.

the see n' sayist. the speak & spellator. the unstrategic essayist[5] with unmitigated disguise: the armored gall of a "poet"

ibid.

[1] references houngan as a time-honored profession.

[2] codeswitch for *fuck your villanelle*

[3] see, *"fried ice cream is a reality"*

[4] see, *"the piccolo player is a motherfucker"*

[5] *"hello 9-1-1? there's a black man with*
a threatening smile & informal prose
in my favorite poetry journal."

Bang

some slick black decay this combustible
decadence this slimy filthy dwarf star collapsing
the organic universe in deep decomposition
my nappy head across your lap

everything that death touches becomes wet.
everything that death touches dehydrates.
everything that death touches inflates and heaves.
everything that death does makes an example of.

a fine layer of dust upon the surface of this vast
oceanic decay. death... defying ripple. a black hole
full of self & a variety of throbbing. the black bang.
the black hole in final implosion. blackly chaotic.
the harvesting of epochs. a temple made of this rippling
cataclysm. the black hole in the throes of death.
vomiting the woes of new life. the destabilizing power
of new love. of stardust made reanimate.
stardust becoming pillow talk. this affliction of life
affirmed. quickly now, as rehearsed: get on top.
slow it down. ride it out. everything that death touches
arches our backs. the final spinal. the body doubles
and becomes a spindle of light / a planet's weight
(minus trajectory) and you allow me to sleep here,
an extinction level event in your crevice of arms and legs.
a hollowed temple. our hearths swaying. reclaiming
everything once considered hallowed. recovery
will take us centuries from now.

two planets in corrected orbit.
every cardinal position its own magnetic pole.
mountains of sky crawling out of skin.

everything that death touches increases yearning
together in rapturous nocturne this sinkhole
a late night carousel of celadon, an ancient hedonism
our holy carousal with teeth in flesh in lissome occult
tails & tongues / vow for vow.

everything that death touches becomes forgiveness
everything that death touches begs for more
everything that death touches increases god
it abandons gloom, this everything we are.

Kizzy Declares To A Customs Agent

admire the speedometer as you wish
with your chassis up high on cinderblocks
and your flintsone feet in full spin cycle

submit your flightplan / update your visa
the entire world is open before you
"meet me in the mountains" says a tea cup

and it's true, not all who wander are lost
but for us who linger / with dreams anchored
in the dawn, anvils for dress socks with locs

weighted down from 40 decades of war
our living tongues made into limestone when
villains flooded the valleys, burning our

boats to ash / of course, the mountains await
once hands are cleansed and museums turned ark

Help Me Get The Body In The Trunk

most often they prefer words that rollercoaster
the lip - the language of loop de loop in verdigris, neon, crayon

anecdotes in braille of busty queens clad in seaweed
and clam shells from the Amazon, ghazal form preferred.

dare to err on the side of Africa then tripe had best
distend in voice's self-study - palms up for hand-outs,

devout to the endearment of others / an ivory towered
endangerment from a thesis-driven drug-habit.

err on the side of self-subsidy and you
will be escorted to a rehab center

by shuttle van with windows tinted - submerged
into another culture's self-absorption; told that your idea

of Africa is not authentic, too romantic and does not yet
represent prerequisite drought, decay, or postmodern

de-colonialism. not that I don't like verdigris or
rollercoasters or loop de loops: I do. but sometimes

the sideshow does not want the funhouse distortion
of mirrors; does not want the slide deck, the theme pitch

or the reflection of Main Street's predisposed astral-projections:
the Mali Kingdom's Street Sweeper Uniform unjustly profiled

as an imitative monkey-suit for our "universal" multi-culture;
I am not amused and don't share such assessments for my

ancestral heritage. you see, I come from a long line of long lines:
the sky split its inseam and out spilled Earth, ocean, and solar flare.

poems that resonate with my daddy's gruff guffaw & mama's
hymnal hum; life-songs, love-songs, rap-songs, sonnets; dirges

that excrete rainbow where the black embrace is thickest
with myth, matriarchy, self's dark authority. trust, too,

that my own desires are canonical, nestled in the ochre of folklore
and can willfully distinguish (when necessary) the differences

between silver lining and razor's edge. I lounge around in kenté,
a close-knit language. who are you to say my agbada is less

a poet's appropriate attire than the silken gowns of Aeschylus,
Epimenides, or Yeats? my dialog deemed disingenuous

when speaking from remote spirit instead of from psyche
through nasal passages. I stare into the throat of my own

supernal phenomena bloated with tinsel and whimsy / gravel and
tragic comedy. this, sir, is my tale, not yours.

beneath such a firmament this voice is as flint casting shadows
and light / creating fire, an opus; legends, lesions, baubles and

bullshit. my voice is a grease-fire, and like yours:
some smoke,   some mirror.

Extra Celestials

- i -

my song: a black tolkien / some solar fare
for the subway away from the middle passages
of a riddled earth

in the inner space of black kisses,
preplanned / omened, our manned flight
spans white distances, saturn's halo
orbits the sankofa between us
our conjoined keloids a constellation
never before named / how else
should we begin? it's a primary propulsion;
let the boosters fall where they may.

the story thus far: i'm your totem
for our remainder of life - tombstone and time capsule
my elegy for us full of turmeric and nanites
the event horizon for a cosmic love - veins
pulse and throb, a sci-fi full of exotic threnodies
and special sauces / we are a single-combustion
chamber full of liquid propellants.

- ii -

simple swam to the shore and found his familiar surface...
a Titan or the Titanic, it all sounds Greek to me;
up wit's creek (or at least its puddle).
muddled mythologies, a newfound tale full of wrought
melanin and tractable meanings: the folklore a foregone

like never before / the final frontier, tangible -
and like Ol' Mother Butler said:

The Blacker The Roddenberry
The Sweeter Its Puce

Orisha Obsidious

Instructions for sequencing:
a always start with *a*
b (or *d*. or *b* & *d* if not *c*)
c (with or without *b*)
d (see instructions for *b*) or go straight to *e* if no *d*.
e always end with *e* or else *e**.
*to be read a stand alone
(for trained initiates only!)

a -
this embryo of dark / black space spiral / virile
midnight swirling / this onyx wet and non-unctuous
vaginal and oleaginous this / this magnetic venom rancid
with non-white wonder / rancid with non-white vocabulary
self-servile, reverse-transcendent - pagan and perversely
reported with discarded veins throbbing in black
omniscience / chews its own adventure.

b -
this
lacquered
language

c -
this golem of ink with tendril-tongue and transient
discourse / this slithering earth with his hoarse whisper / his
umbral rasp / this gawlo with the guttural non-growling ghetto
within visceral skin, living & cognitive

d -

how does one even consider the abridgment
of black holes a possibility? ... / ... beware the man
with unicorn meat in his entrails, his spells are
a constellation collapsing / coils of moonlight & fairie skulls
are kept in his festering apothecary, his dictionary a ghost quarry
this   Orisha Obsidious
this Hoodie-Endangerment
with avalanche packed in ears, his totemic eyes
leaking mudslide on the floors of an ancestral
abyss but you will never romanticize his wizardry
his wonderments / this wrought & iron witch / this
healer with an african face leaning into cold climates
to uphold the wind / he spindles dawn
drenching what-we-think-we-know in brightest day

in a world dismayed with lightlessness, our Hero,
this Black Start Diesel hoards the horizon, indentured
to covetous eclipse with raw, nocturnal aura...
this Igbonic man / more than flora
with opaque indices waning the profane
        you feel his love

//////////////////////////// and yet \\\

e -

        you still refuse it.

Bysshe, Please

face it

you brought us here for a reason / just the one:
to be caretakers for a lechery made non-linear

the stage-hands for pay-per-viewed debauchery
batting clean-up after bacchanalia / made stoic

within frames and labeled still life
for the walls of your hoodang / yodeling odes

to Ozymandias / our bodies bound & unbound
like golems stashed in closets & cages (unquietly-as-kept)

so what's it like to mass produce a zombie horde
for your beck & call lurching under cloak

under-educated, under foot & over-docile / and not once
have you ever thought to not own us / not once

have you liked us / not sincerely / not once / not even
for the well-heeled, doe-eyed literates / although

for us "good ones"

a Norse Code was given / "bequeathed"
it's called like gold stars in grade school

trophies of elocution for your most precious darkies:
the embrace of neon after the alphabet.

we've entered your throes-of-death wanted of us
this controlled coin toss with holocausts clashing

you wanted it / your implicit thought: this is what
they get for thinking / how niggardly you are

with your secession of lambskins / vellums worn
like academic chevrons in defense of your hood

but let's face it / it's not an unknown

a glittering Sir Gawain hovering above
the stable hand with doo rag and thick lip:

> "behold, King Primate," (*your forebearers*
> *proclaiming once to ours*) "this
>
> ever-lashing life / a fumigation from
> the proclivities that damn you
>
> you poor soulless mule droning on and on
> of your inconsequential wounds
>
> you man-made misanthrope with your

maladroit songs decomposing on your lips

go & worship your tinny drums with your dusty
hands / but let their tiny ditties offer praise

only to your masters / after all, nigger,
your breed ain't metaphysical."

the sainted science vs the fetish faith

we see it now, all, so simply / so yes
incontrovertibly / yes / if only on paper:

one of us must surely die.

my hope was to write a sonnet wet enough
to drown you / elbow to nape

your mouth a dehiscent romance gulping
your gills wrenched of lasting wrath

but even in death we know the critics
from your childhood will be lenient

your corpse wreathed as a higher feat
the debut of your garbage bin turned

palatial estate / the venue where you

launder money flipped into a museum

or endowment / but if you demise into
a poem is it still considered murder?

this specious god made
into a precious metal.

please i implore, submit to this sentencing
for we all are tired... and it's your turn to hang

but even then: from your dying harangue
from your crock of shit - a flock of sparrows

your rancid breath a rainbow with
hollywood at your gilded door

begging for your decaying dirge / your joys
and tears turned canon fodder (if not the law

or acts of faith) / my mother's femur
like flotsam in your wake of shadows and yet

here i am / fragmented and rent above you / this wail
for the ages / my holy gourds above your grails

my romanticism for the cairns & slivers &
the dark-hued revenants that haunt you

re-animators of the most visibly cleft / this
angry narcissistic poet with a God(Damn)

Complex / Mr Hyde / The Hood hulked up
on a bag of skittles and a wee spot of tea

forgive me.

the initial snap of noose left my brogue
bereft of flora and only my fervid eczema

remains evidently verdant:

1. my indecorous decree with unintended gurgle
2. the bold orthopedic boot with discomfit insole
3. this musculature of staples & grafted sinew
4. the voltaic arcs dripping in full array
   from fingertips / "urrrgh, aargh!" / all

conveying what the distance gave us.

the black hole tilts weeping comets & cataclysms
from its canthus: ancestral bodies bright & celestial

the likes of which we forbid you to name

so, yes // exactly
this // only this // that sonnet
as it was promised:

the two-fold saga plays itself out / the townfolk
        quickly turning / the pale dewy milk-maid with her
pitchforks aflame / the professor-poet of frail
        ego and angry doctorate / the cleric with
his leash & lash & classic english / the smoking
        jackets / the tiki torches / only Igor hemmed
& hawed: the warning signs / the symptoms / all there / now
        all is lost / we honed a catalyst / canaries;
heralds for this percussional distance: Robert
        Hayden / Gwendolyn Brooks / Octavia Butler
Margaret Walker / legions, a host... so many
        ledgered agents / their plumes a Night-Scented incense;
they set themselves in flames and you didn't listen.
        you nev.... (sigh)   -   *even the hunchback saw it coming*

you mastered flame now
all's ash / the woe, the wonder.
Mary Shelley - she,

                she tried to warn you.

Modern Xenomorph

for the sake of a new make & model
the mouth is made a tool & die / volts

of black bolt through the porcelain above
the clouds are red with light & laughter

the crackle of doom spares nothing
begets a cackle of dawn behind the ribs

our tongues spackled with runes & anger
this auger of self-awareness

the danger of some long-dormant spoor
in a thing long-thought dead / this lesion

of spring in the silos of winter
(invasions from a body snatched)

iron bars staple shut the gaping hole
as black thesis in the borrowed patient's

wounded chest a solder of stitches
as a dark art holding the stolen heart

in steady place once reanimated
the gods discover deficiencies in fire

they fuck & deliver children on embers
a mountain of coal for a furnace of figments
language is a rampageous gel
on the thickest of lips

apologues gorging on
the forge of molten tongue

arms out, hands extend the distance
and witness, beneath his nails: all the earth.

Liyongo is the Titan
no one talks about.

To Have The Wish I Wish Tonight

1 / 5
to float as pollen above the hive
arms flared embracing this precipice of air
the wrought iron of the short rail upon which i lean
digging into thigh above knee until a trickle of blood
(bloodpollen)
the unentangled body as heavy as a man
or pregnant woman tethered around the nape
a diaphanous floating stain / a silhouette
that hovers within history like an angry wasp
trapped in your upturned jelly glass...
its stinging litigation a dead man's wish:
to be startlingly bright, a star falling through
the pixelating heat of an August moon
searching for the sweet center of a fig

2 / 5
the haze is a crow around us / corpulent
with famine and neglect: praisesongs for the strips
of carrion under caw asking how much
the horizon weighs / as much as a golem?
a gorilla? a 400 pound pupa? we become
and unbecome / the surreal made to discomfort

your eyes are a mineshaft collapsing; or
as hazel suns   yes, still   collapsing.
from the haze there is blood in our tears; then
told it's from our nature always veering into anger.

when asked for freedom they gave us its concept.

3 / fifths
let's say you cut a buzzard open

not politely (bear with me) as a christmas ham
but for the museum of it to see how its carcass shines
from inside out its viscus of many facets / with
the great winds coagulating in its lungs / your poking,
your prodding as curator for a tour of entrails

what, by the way, is the asking price
for public access to another being's hunger pang?
to open a dark, drying body like a shadow box
dissecting appetite / flagged pins piercing
through feathers & skins flayed aside,
demarcations for morbid gps - "you are here.
...& you are here. ...& ...& ...are you ever not here?"

tiny placards that impale intestine // what
ley lines exist beneath the heart of another being
broken in half for curiosity / for amusement / for
the sake of science! for the strength of convictions
inherited... how deeply must you dig
to reach a crossroads? less than an inch? more
than a fathom? the lump in the buzzard's throat
a ball of dirt / a mood ring of dull fading thirst...

then (goddammit, i said bear with me!), then
each morsel vacuum packed for prosperity,
in perpetuity as birthright to serial progeny....
the buzzard's beak deemed a thing of beauty,
another cultureless tchotchke for the mantel

in 400 feet your destination is on the right.

beguiling isn't she:
the siren voice of the google map assistant
her song a Manifest Cartography / you know,
she exists only to absolve the driver of any

guilt / for their rage / for their roadkill / for
their many turns wrongly taken
always behind the wheel / a Child of Muir
lost in reckless wander, until when told
to retrace your steps / you've gone too far

4 / 5
the wrought iron surrenders
against the thigh, iron rivets wobbling
in their loose, crumbling sockets / our entire bodies
unbraced and unafraid of the freefall - how long
has our flaring streak looped against heaven - if
stones, this mere gravel, (as if stars) scattered
across this dry barren earth   can be heaven.

I

the black body is a biodegradable poem;
the lines of each stanza begins as they end:
the canopy above is too small to contain

Here, The Earth Giant Dreams Himself A Cloud

my proclivities are the soft
umbral opening of mouth
in unmetered prayer // not you / no
unnecessary ibid at the tale end
of this treatise / i will not be
referenced away / i stand within time atop time
like a self-replicating genesis

the goal?

for centuries to pass / my piled bones
bleached with sun / for my muse
stygian & corpulent / her heavenly heft
atop my skull / akonting on her knee weeping
nostalgiac for our Talons Of Love / her wings
heavy and wet from tears / her limbs a soft river of woe
enfolding with thick lips & opulent tongue aquiver
recalling my name

and this is how the everlasting comes to me:

> with stirring winds
> a trembling leaf

Pell Grant For A Space Force

(a sonnic)

i roll up in the buff, a ball of wolves,
at your window / to your door; i'm cardboard
& cobalt: like a blues / my banjo is
a cigar box, a jumble of old bra
straps & three strands of mountain locs for strings.
my head is carved from wood / a poro mask
with kokoshnik crown; words stacking within
words like a canopic jar / or seeds within
a pomegranate / my love for you is
the dead wasp at the center of a fresh,
budding fig; can i woo you with kisses
contaminating / lisp laminating
skin? your putty left impressed / concussed by
the inks seeping until that settles that;
tea steeped in honey. all i'm saying is
watch as i pull a habit from this rat
or from some other broken stanza made
prone from depreciating similes;
the night sky pouring through my windows like
a faucet / stars pooling at feet. it's like i'm
Władziu Valentino Liberace
and Patrice Lumumba's lovechild for you;

candomblé meeting candelabra in
        the wild and in this sentence the engine
stalls: my emperor has no clothes / no one
        has more no clothes than he! come & see what
the most least looks like / language devoid of
        lingerie; like you, i was born in an
alternate banality / i'm anti-
        fascist and it keeps raining ketchup / no
wonder we're american. but i'm not
        a peeping tom. i'm only here for the
kidnapping, grab your coat / the ransom note
        written in crayons & sausage gravy
so authorities take me serious.
        "here be dragons" begins our wedding vows.

this cocooning dawn
soft and coy in my callused
hands embracing hips

lover, if there's a vacancy for a
        make-believe-friend, let me in. if i eat
you up i'll lit you out, i swear / isn't
        the cryptozoologist in you just
a little bit curious? and should all
        else fail, then trade with jack: my magic beans
for that tawny cow / skin the cat, collect
        the bounty / return to sender and don't

look back: i'll always be waiting; the moth
drawn to contagion / the giant-slayer
with the golden goose grin / your driver of
the stretch limo stage coach with the sweet, low
haberdashing trash-talk; burn the bridge or
download my app / i'm always combusting;
the lycanthrope with the listerine smile.
beneath this tangerine's rind, near its core,
my whole heart, holding hope, bleating your name.
my heart, a ruby; a hole in rubble.

Dirt Farmer

poems should live off the land
should hunt and kill sinking its teeth
into something with bigger teeth than it...

not blood-thirst; has nothing to do
with hunting for fun; should not
harbinger sociopaths under its similes...

poems should grow whole societies
from a single cell / from drops of blood,
from the chaffed seed...

not that our verbs should be against
the cold-blooded-kill... reaping is at times
the best weapon sanitizing insanity.

i'm just fucking with you
i'm just pontificating;
nothing more / nothing less:

why no writer any longer tends
trending toward the roots
of black-agricultural-consciousness.

I want poems
that raises pigs
before it grills them.

Cul-De-Sac Safari

welcome to your 2020 White Safari Safety Manual

warning: social changes happen quickly, without notice;
please refresh your browser every 15 seconds for updates.
in case of a power outage please open a channel
to your local deity.

1
the neon flashes:
keep arms within vehicle at all times
it is never day; dawn is always coming

2
the television is not your tribe.
it will kill you; your assassination archived
for youtube / labeled not safe for work

do not attempt to watch and ride

3
batten down the hatches:
unless you are finn the human
your hoodie is never above half-mast
and loosely fastened to see
your clean-shaven smile
but keep just in case
your standard-issue white-face
within easy reach

to demonize the black face
fascism needs a dark, blank canvas
to avoid being mistaken the clay pigeon
apply the wite-out - liberally (don't laugh!)
around the lips (this will be addressed
in better light later)

4
tretorns, nu balance, or vans?
here are wildebeest in the suburbs
much faster than tigers and lions
and everyday can be a track meet;
life is the marathon they make it
and every single step must be divisible
by the 100 yard dash

street cred
does not apply...
please duct-tape
your jumpmans
responsibly

5
- a
mcdonald's being a safespot is a trap!
poachers rim the lot for easy prey
anywhere you see a golden arch
is an elephant graveyard

- b

every man-of-the-cloth
is a dark decoy; if even the pope
asks for directions try this stalling tactic:
scrunch your face with the black-hand side
of your hand on your hip the other hand
scratching your nape with your right foot
askance and say "geez, feller, you got me."

- c

the homeless man on
the ronald bench is a secret ranger,
he is there to rescue; drop any coin
into his cup to activate

allies-in-states-of-emergency only

they are trained as human shields
who historically organize the marches
bereaved on your behalf

6

do not stare down the rubberneckers.
they seek a riot in your eyes...
also, do not stare into your cellphones
or stare at clouds in self-reflection
the wild seek your attention
but they must not see you taking notice

this is where you are most in danger

7

even if it's as hot as the Sudan
do not stop to fan yourself
make no sudden moves
the non-native natives will mistake
sudden shifts in normality as gang-signs
watch the ways their lips realign
as they google your color combinations
heed the rift as it opens between you

8

the locals might not
know to like you and might be
militia-minded; elmer fudd
owns a mansion & a yacht
and is always hunting wabbits

9

this is no time, Black Millennials,
to abandon MotherWit, sipping tea
and throwing shade for snapchat
so be careful with your cameras:
filming by cellphone is a superstition
invoking anger & confusion / they fear
(in their culture) the lens
capturing their inner goals

if they advance fall prone & curl
into a ball do not call for help
do not whelp for passersby
to protect you because they too
can be souvenir collectors.

do not display anger
(or laughter or too much hope)
pray the sudden danger passes
and if one runs up to you
with spittle in speech and
nostrils flared then stand still
as shit / our grandmothers
all told us to stand still as fuck

this is sometimes, sadly,
the only way a second class
perception survives
a first world phantasia

10
if you must run decide quickly -
this is not the moment for soft reflection.
when walking, ALWAYS note your
escape routes. flinching can be fatal
so when the moment comes
                              haul ass!
knock over every trash can

in passing; cut corners.
in fact, when cutting corners
do not cut corners,
this is vital

11
"officer friendly"
is a concrete figment.
universal law here
is a grand illusion.
if it has a badge
then it is holding its breath
and it's fear will bravely
teethe upon you.
if it's an officer, then chances are
it is already deciduous
& seething.

12
in self-defense, if you fight,
pick up a brick and knock
the living shit out of your pursuer.

please, do not stop!

among their pack you have already
been prosecuted
their fear is very fertile

and to them you are always
on foreign soil
among their tribe
you have no rights.

whatever you do, don't
let them track you
to your mother's house.
or your bloodlines
will all be made undone.
woman or child, your closest kin
will all know cages within cages.
even if you are pacifist
be prepared to kill
or they will only come back
with swat teams and
camera crews with news
anchors boo-hooing
on their behalf
threatened by the spectacle
of their own eyes / blinking

13
yes: run or fight: either way,
there will be consequences.
your innocence is
out of their question;
there is jail or

there is death or
there is jail-death
so, never leave home
without visas and
dual citizenship papers
historically there is canada
for those in the north
and if you safari
in the south you can always
swim in a pinch
to cuba

14

2 FIELD NOTES ON SURVIVING SAFARI

\- i -

every sidewalk's a cautionary
tale of two cities / never adventure
alone! hire a guide and a good lawyer;
someone adept in the commerces of
tom sawyer and great gatsby, in mockingjays
and mockingbirds, in raven quotes and
wind-up birds, giant peaches, in wizards
and warlocks, in sneetches and well-seasoned
witches... but if he or she recites fight
clubs, atlas shrugs or philosophies in
fisticuffs, then shut it down for they have
red-eye crine tricks & not the droids you seek.

\- ii -

if you do go it alone, then only
carry backpacks, never a 'nations bag
or croaker sack! take these supplies for swap
or bribe: a pound of brie and a bottle
of wine, a moleskin, any vonnegut,
most bukowski, the beatles (white album)
but don't offend for some have sensitive
ways - if things go awry, just back away
if possible, without blinking, without
ever having seen eye to eye - just leave
the james joyce and emily dickinson
tributes: like good fruit in picnic baskets.

15

if you drive, if pulled over,

DO NOT GET OUT OF YOUR VEHICLE.

in this situation,
"keep your hands inside the ride at all times"
is kinda sketchy. some are said
to have survived, but these are rumors
and all reliable surveillance says otherwise.

the good book or the green book
both are full of lies

16

stay hydrated.
but more importantly
stay out of florida,

arizona, much of
the deep south, most
of the upper north...

the midwest... texas... the west west...
hawaii? still to be determined...
if you safari

in one of those lands,
then let a loved one know
far in advance.

we know you must get to school,
to work, to the daycare, the
grocery store and that walking,

the bus, the subway, your own car,
flight, and even teleportation
has its dangers...

we know that simply standing
comes with limitations
when you safari in america

but please be careful.
be more careful than
is humanly possible
be damn near
omniscient in the cautions
you dare take...

17

remember / remember:

your life is always at stake & maybe your pride but in general it doesn't
hurt to slur your feet across the earth keep a 70s dictionary of slang
in a glovebox carry persimmons & mangoes & kale chips carry a song
in your heart & your heart on your sleeve perhaps you should learn a
dance like the moonwalk or the running man or the milly rock carry
your wallet in a white girl walking ten paces ahead carry a tin of
shoe polish in your fannypack with the wite-out in case of worst case
scenarios in case of worst case scenarios multiply by 3 and carry the 1
pray to switchblades and be a machete in the shadows of the people you
love should you not come to safari to linger then practice beforehand a
liberating art like levitation or the colonizing skills of the taxidermist
sharpen your fangs dear sweet lion and be a hunter big in the game with
room in your hallways for the collection of heads your roaring memoir
(as theirs) a textbook for victors:

remember / remember.

Psalm For An Underexcavated Hum

everywhere beyond the bed is an unnecessary tundra
this sore and sticky hibernation. the snuggle.
this continuous spooning that never seems to run dry.
and you've made a cave of me. a hollowed out colossal
with this long overdue spring running hot in my november skin.
a ravenous cavern. black & calcified. always aqueous.

Abstrack Africana No. 15

there are 44 million of us to this forest,
a flood zone / a shifting waterfall / we are
a small migratory moon tilting the sea

upfromsumdirt Applies For A Job

work experience:

i am spirit-machine / 3 centuries of soapstone and cowrie shell and post-modern mythical technology / mine's is a digital rasp / i'm a son of shango and not a son of shaft or the lovechild of the mr. bojangles i-phone app many of you want me to be / 7 generations removed, i am an ashanti king-wannabe in dada sneakers shooting dice for ramens money between the black muslim mosque and the used bookstore that was once a whites-only museum / only my tongue is temple / a collection plate of black consciousness / séance as equally sacred as science / according to a long-lost voodoo calendar i was borne in the year of the zombie / i am spirit-machine / machine-gun-runner-supreme / there is afrosheen in my circuitry / my nano-sciences glow and they gleam / my motherboard teems with songs-to-honor-the-dead-by / the shoes of the fisherman's wife is some jive ass slippers is my theme-song / the entire junior kimbrough discography is a rotating ringtone / and elegba beatboxes in my voicemail / i'm forever rhyming under rubble / squeezing blood from the blues (and when lucky / from its titties) / i live on and on / the living loop sample for the ancestors / but even Don Cornelius ages and i have yet to have The Sons and Daughters of Nat Turner follow back when i heart-thingie all of their posts on instagram / i'm really distraught over that / i may need therapy / or in the very least a sincere hug / or a good cry over black coffee / i am spirit-machine / a ghost of malcolm x-mas past / egungun ex machina / but i work well with others & need zero supervision to complete a task.

things about myself i'd like to improve:

i harbor a grudge. and would like to
remove the elmer fudd tramp stamp
tattooed on my back... and brussels sprouts –
i'd like to eat a fuckin' brussel, just once, like
a goddamn adult (i'm 52, for god's sake!)
i'd like to hotwire a police car after robbing a bank
and maybe die cinematically in a hail
of gunfire after kidnapping the banker's
daughter and maybe not be bludgeoned
to death for eating a bag of skittles or
for pulling out my cellphone for selfies
outside the police officers' ball.
to be remembered as a poet. another
black assed motherfuckin' poet. and
maybe i could, for just a day, marry
for good credit instead of all this
redemptively engrossing storybook love.

Engine Block Feng Shui For Boy Davis' Only Son

to tell the truth,

if you ever believed in 'magical negroes', then Daddy
was your man, a regular trapeze-artist/zen-master/slave-tradin'
train-robber-baron who rode side-saddle with bill pickett, genghis
khan, nat love, and idi amin.

goosed mary todd beneath her corset and shot lincoln dead
in his stove-top while pushing broom at ford's theater before
pinning the rap on that passing pansy john wilkes booth.

single-handedly, he shipwrecked the titanic; stowed away
on apollo 14 and (i swairfogawd!) clocked his best friend dead
in the jaw for calling martin luther king an uncle tom coon.
beat a jackstopper down for calling the prince of peace
a picaninny-pauper.

rumor has it, when archeologists was rummaging through
tutankhamen's dirty draws, they dug up Daddy, his shadow trapped
in a sarcophagul crease by an old witch's evil spell. Daddy roared up
/ a red-eyed hairy man choking down beef tongued ladyfingers
and drinking pabst from mr. bojangles' sweaty boot.

Daddy wore a zoot suit. once. but typically he just walked around
in white boxers, a v-neck tee, and wing-tips with tassels. kisses
were communal property; never came home in the same shoes twice.

Daddy wasnt a rollin' stone but a rock collector. kept his curio
full of canadian mist and other people's house keys. victoria's
secret stayed pickled in ohio river brine in mason jars on the mantel.
motor oil fermented under fingernails, every household mirror
reflected his image, even when he wasnt home.

there were no witnesses, but when he passed away they say the devil
piously came paying Him respect and paved paths away
from the gates of hell. you see,
there are no vacancies for villain-saints like Daddy in the lower levels

besides, undocumented incorporeal workers like him lived rent free.
not that Daddy was an angel - pfft! - far from it! it's just
jesus owed him silver for driving judas home drunk after
the first water-to-wine routine didn't go as planned, he offered Pops
salvation as payment after the son of god's celestial check bounced.
He hocked gabriel's horn until all sides of the occult settled up.
but typically, for your john hancock to end up
in Groundhog's Golden Ledger
meant you was caught out casting lots and stones at the glass homes
of magical-negro-nonbelievers. found yourself ground under
some wailing road and not even sister harriet herself
could conduct you to freedom.   shit happens.
and god forbid your self-belief should jam up at the crossroads
and you had to call Daddy for a helping hand:

"that's on you, son; what the fuck can I do about it?"

but then there He'd be:

knocking simon legree dead on his ass, his meaty valvolined fingers
all up in the apparels of pauline; the peril lifted and you left
holding the bag, pulling up the caboose.

but where others failed, Daddy would help see you through;
after first of course rolling His eyes and spitting
pabst blue ribbon in your general direction.
but whichever way - you can't not carry it:

His smile your favorite scar, pushing you
2 steps ahead of wherever your life stalled.

Mr. Greaseball Slick; Kentucky's Head as Hard as
a Rock of Gilbralter / Rother... *"no middle name"*...

...shaming the devil.

A Small Poem To Let You Know The End Is Near

enjoy the stillness, this serene
comfort where thick, luscious
moss grows over the scars on
our backs; the wounds of which
are now a modern currency.

A Time Unraveller's Travel Journal

Day 1

entry:
back in the days of yore, the Consortia of Erebus dissected the testicles of Chronos treated time like an 8-track and turned modern-day physics into Doctor Who's private prostitute / you can now drop a dime into the slots of any ol' time-machine and get whisked into the infancies of man / our entire past repackaged as a brand new day.

entry:
now I don't know much about chronology / i sweep the streets in this twenty-fifth century Kentucky town but like all "civil servants" trapped in diaspora my gourds have kept their secrets here in this ustaarabu bandia but if I too could go back in time I'd be the tattletale and run my mouth to every Sahel mystic or Songhai imperialist in sight goddammit / i'd ride the night on the back of a camel cryin'

"the Portuguese, the Dutch, and the British are comin'!"

entry:
well, I do have keys to the Consortia's lab / I'm a cheguevaraist with a janitorial degree never been one for Chronos but Sankofa is another story / i'd create schisms and undo chaos / i'd go back and cause change rearranging every vicious accord / yes i'd revise the records and slap the hands of prim alabaster gloved in lavender and limestone line-breaking reconstruction what an entertaining thought:

could I really go back and sink La Santa Maria?

entry:
scalping Columbus takes high credentials leaving no one the wiser /
cutting the guts out of John Smith / shit maybe gloved alabaster
already did it: according to some theorists a Mali scientist may have
slept at the wheel and left the hood up on quantum physics allowing the
disdaining sons of Europe to unravel afrocentric superpowers turning
all of black history into a newly oppressed people's hoodoo / such
explains why beneath two feet of snow there is always three
feet of tar / perhaps with one fell swoop I could undo
this dire entireness / this apocalyptic conundrum /
this plague of apoplexy.

entry:
but could I be the hero for Our Beautifully Dark Hordes™
and still be holed up in this bottom?

entry:
could i surrender it all just to be a superhero in secret? going down as
the miracle worker and be The World's Most Elaborately Immaculate
Unknown Martyr?

entry:
and of the consequences? is nonexistence the fare for a selfless sacrifice
and what of my family?

my wife.

my children.

if I change a time-line would that include our love would I erase
every memory and tender moment? could I?
would that mute every leaning of us into us / exchanging new
but unknown destinies for the near certainty of
dust-to-dust rendering moot my own propriety /
my morality / my rightful-mindedness? could I be so willing
dragging shadows into the dark just to save
my people un-enslaved? I mean nothing
is more important than my family but if I re-dress today in dashikis
instead of cummerbunds *would I* in turn *wither away and die?*

I don't wanna die

but i tire paying licensing fees for daylight to those disingenuous with dawn / no one inherits the sun if they are silent with history

I'll sleep on it and hope i don't betray myself in slumber (bluetoothed pillows are standard-issue and connect wirelessly to the NSA / an uncle once in a dream stole silver and the Trancing Authority mistook his nocturnal monologue as confessions of guilt / spent 17 months in chains until he was cleared 'unconvicted' they called it) - but it sounds like my decision is made

yes. I think this is the done deal.

entry:
my teleportation transfer ticket has expired for today so no scooting home across the stratosphere with double helixes scattered then piecemealed some eighty miles away and no unlicensed jetpacking after dark / I could take a horse & buggy but have you seen the cost of apples or sugarcane - Ten Broeck Goddam! & just try feeding a cube or two of sweet-n-low to a shetland pony / let's see how far that gets you.

Day 4

entry:
can't take iron into the past so black words will be my remedial rifle but it's not anger not even angst just tired of the disenfranchised indifference where the whites of their eyes roll at 'black power' slogans where real liberation is the loudest winter and I'm so tired of all of this fuckin' winter being on my permanent record

I never learned liking the taste of drought and in most societies there are seasons for torrential rains / earthy grains for harvest / I want my people to fall back into the earth spreading arms and legs freely / making sun-angels in the grass fingers flirting with every green shaft remembering how good "good" feels...

entry:
or 'greatness' when's the last time we talked about black greatness without deferring to athletes & soul singers / some idol worshippers all of us sending text-praises to Saint Simon our great digital calf / his

head hangs in the Smithsonian / disco-balls for eyes / Sinatra's first gold hit sits aureola-like behind him - it's creepy / many times I've had to clean it.

entry:
800 years of post-slavery trauma / an overly-dramatic dysfunction that sociologists claim is our innate state / that it's in our dna to be a
natural danger with penchants for awakening as the strangers to
ourselves dreamed up by Darwin but damn him and
the orangutan he rode in on / once I open up
the worm-hole I'll rewrite this evolutionary
synthesis proving to the Agnostics there was never inertia to
the Tertiary World that black socio- sedimentarialism
does not equate to sedentary lifestyles that
educated guessing does not validate the side-effects of slavery /
that the "freedom to amuse" does not replace a free man's need
for mules or many many acres or for many muses all one's own.

entry:
maybe I have some anger. my every word ruined with resentment and shaved on soapstone until sharp and stainless / my undocumented Sankofa a real soft shank / but if I do reverse time and I change every event since then then I'm going to miss Basquiat's art and Baldwin's words and Bearden's cut-ups / if only I alone am left to remember then I'll emote a long low moan for Muddy Waters a round of whiskey black coffee for Eunice Waymon: libations for a better living and a fuller liberty.

entry:
of course there are papers to sign permissions to be gained liability waivers to be signed and visa applications approving time travel with valid reasons to go unchaperoned / can't request jaunting through jolts of time with thunderbolts peering from my fannypack / I'll hafta play it cool act calm and charm the custodians of Novikov's self-consistency principle so that I'm allowed to roam unfettered tethered only to my own grand allusions.

entry:
don't want to create the parallel paradox / I wanna be free not just feel free / back in 2235 we all moved to Canada but A Beautiful Batuque
called us back / there was still Congo in Kentucky - it was
on a t-shirt / we even had a long-running sitcom about
the heroes of The Third Civil Rights Movement / all to no end
but disastrous results / i mean even the loss in beehives didn't
matter so what was all this chatter about Black Lives?
our textbooks still said: *"And God opened the gangplanks*
and all the blacks emerged in origin / battered scratched and
scarred / hatching from the rafter's searing heat of Heaven's
un-cosmic cargo bay / these faceless phantasms disembarked
into a second class genesis lasting for all time /
but from the benevolence that broke them they learned to sing for their supper and made some really great music / from the Blessing-Of-Our-Demand for their appearance of servility they gifted us their free will (orthey died) and it was good / Amen / so fuckin' much Amen, everybody!"

entry:
it's unhuman not to hate them.

entry:
I suppose I have to move on / behooving time to put this plan into action / I'll return some 400 years ago to see if I can elect a black man with a suspicious pedigree president of the former first world / the first test of a dry-run / maybe I'll esteem the black occult as was done with Mt Olympus / I think / yes I can.

entry:
maybe this'll bring the fabled Drum-Corps of Engineers to fruition: a Council of Old Dreads co-signing the past the present the possible the probable and the illogical / a congress of gray locs / representatives / each a century of wisdom Bandits for Father Ptah banded as one disabling historical subterfuge I can see it now:

our black faces on green money one nation under Egun - In Olorun We Trust how dope is that? pure and uncut I'll become John The Conqueroo The First / Concierge for New Alkebulan / the Drum-Corps could host my naming ceremony a djembe-circle with me standing in their ring of honor saluting all the Ancients uncut pure empowerful

Day 12

entry:
my entire life I've been the solid citizen - shovelin' the shit shootin' the breeze to boss hogs and top guns but still a good life cain't say that I personally was played the fool ...a good life

but blacks we look at the entire wreckage not the incremental balms and the sub-sufficient paregorics / my personal life? it is wonderful. but had it not been built upon a mythology of ruin / this citizenship from carnage so thorough and complete / remember when all of Haiti had to pay 80 million dollars to France for freedom? stolen property paid reparations to thieves
thief said:
"we made you niggerkings a thing / suckled honey from your breasts until they bled / wed you to an everlasting cataclysmic system and now you must pay us back for that privilege"
the robber-baron-banking-system / perversions to power / then global change killed the ice caps and Haiti sank into the sea back in 2052 / their flotsam flesh deemed 'a 3rd class pollutant' behind oil spills and floating islands made of plastic.

entry:
we're tired of saying "thank you" to
devastation / ingratiating our

offspring to armageddons
easily avoided / you know for a people
so hung up on the Paperworks O'Liberty and the quantum physics of anarchy why are the whites so angry that their cash cows kept a ledger?

"the times they are a'changin'"

(was Bob Dylan prophesizing me?)

but if I can pull this off then my people will all descend from one
single odalisque / she'll be a royal woman / no mere paramour
but a paragon! the Mother-Muse of all Romanticism
/ her name will be *Olanrewaju* / apotheosis unparalleled /
just you watch / just you wait and see.

Day 16

entry:
it's all really ironic that it took a bush- doctor from Africa
reading Kaku to crack open the universe / how before the
academic elite felt useless and suicidal / so incomplete
& unable to seize the unseen with their sciences
and then Kereenyaga reached into his
'nations sack giving meta- physics a soul / he said:

"lookitchu / done broken down every
galactic grain / sorted, sifted, and strained every
ounce of solar shit examining everything / everything / but 'deepest
darkest Africa' / the Igbo overlooked by layers of lettered ego / but the
universe was never that elusive / you just weren't looking / isn't it
obvious? your missing negative matter? the evidence all aligns if only you
would look: it's the black man / egun ex machina / but what good are

exploits if all are equal, right?"

the key to quantum cosmology came in the curing of sickle cells in the Congolese / at the center of the decayed cancer was the semen of God Itself and thus begat the deification of Kaluza-Klein / all of Sweden received a nobel / all seven dwarves were lauded except Kereenyaga who was mysteriously killed / in Sweden / "skiing" — that fool is now the patron haint for black-skinned braggarts who talk too much while walking ass first into the lion's den when Zwarte Piet was not enuf.

entry: time travel. hyperspace. warp speed.

we've scathed all of physics / left sci-fi in need of stitches / there's a bordello in a black hole / we've given rings to Mars / a bustling Pluto is again a planet / the surface of the sun has a Starbuck's logo that's only seen when rising / the moon has a moon / it's an amazing age this 25th century / Dannon sells a Greek yogurt actually made in the Minoan era (they tell Minos the Yangshao are big on it) / the president of our Ministry of Physics has been a midwife for the births of Plato, Einstein, and Bruce Springsteen / we've been to Heaven and Hell and the Cenozoic Era and yet still we won't go near the ghetto

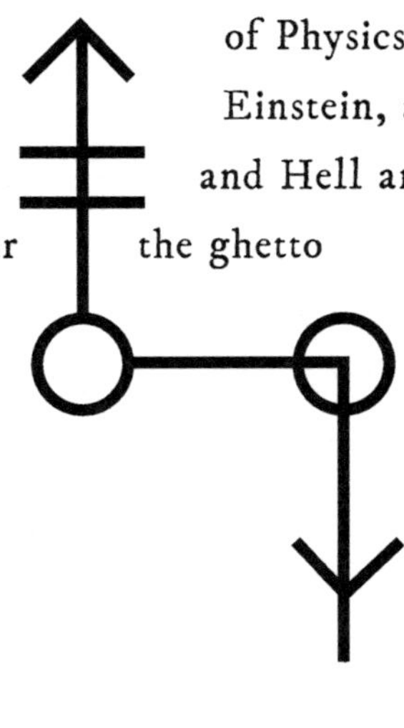

not even for
a nickel bag
of tachyons

unfortunately there's been no tectonic shift in ethics.

Day 19

entry:
Mandela's bust should be on the side of a mountain not just as a tie-dyed silhouette on the face of antiquated currency.

Day 25

entry:
think about it / be honest what noble quest would King Arthur endure just to reclaim his name or honor his throne? Arthur / Doctor Who / Captain Kirk / Superman / Bruce Willis / Bruce Wayne / John Wayne - well Kenya is my Camelot / we too had royal crowns in Ancient Congo / our tales also the stuff of legends & storyboards and despite what classical 20th century cinema says Sam Jackson coulda Died Hard just as well / not like that role required great acting / so yeah / let me go and turn Old Tanzania into a spaghetti western / this is for the dark-hued alchemists / for the goldsmiths hewing blood and dirt into ancestral art / for Tyler Perry as Songhai Gladiator his iconic bronze buffed and shirtless in every scene

couldabeen - shouldabeen

this time the Middle Passage runs straight through Middle Earth leaving orcs and elves to fill the diaspora

"this time / that time / next time"

but first / for now / let me return home to hold my wife because tonight we cherish the day as yesterday (like the old temporal travel agents used to say) is no longer promised / to anyone.

Day 26

entry:
"goodbye, cruel world"

with spear and sneer I'm off / sullen and sound / the spook sitting by the wormhole / steeping into organic darkness for metallic light / this new night in shining armoire pulling cosmic strings / tripping around Tipler's Cylinder until ...embers... soon all of this 'now' is just soot and embers / salting the fields as gravity gives way yielding 'new' / a ceremonious unremembrance to this unrequited twilight / retooling time

"goodbye, grueling world"

farewell to all of this lopsided overruling through hateful words demanding we be grateful graceful and delighted with this infernal servitude void of any finite terminal this can't be our future!

so through cracks in
anatomies of time /
unraveling this hard
I'm only seeking Love /
offered / but after all
question remains: why
now not already know this
commingled — we — these
centuries all?

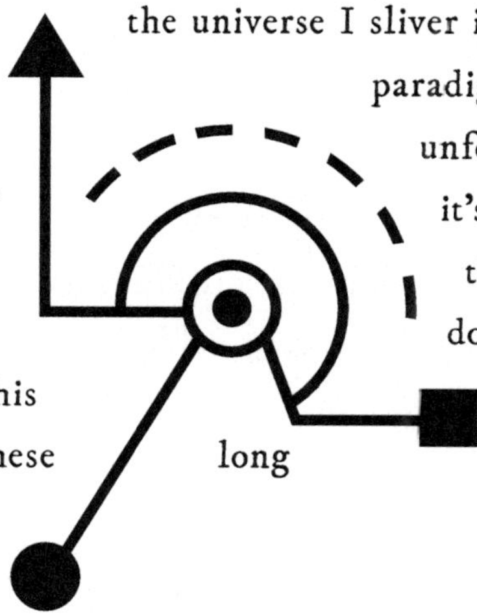

the universe I sliver into the
paradigm traveling /
unforgiving hurt /
it's all we've ever
these eons the
do you here &
of me /
long
cold

A Time Unraveller's Travel Journal: The Sankofa Paradox

the atmosphere swallows you
shatters skin and bone and psyche
7 million layers of skin
seared away
every cell splintered in a single second
the soul split in halves a quarter million times
a hurt so quick and hard it barely tickles

in time travel (for the tourists)
psychologists await on the other side
physicists, physical therapists, multi-linguists,
money lenders, money launderers, and
tour guides...

but you claim the cult of Legba
and your worm-hole is the esophagus
of voodoo traveling through Olodumare's
inner linings, his intestinal tracks
and dark matters.

atmosphere shits you out
landing within lightning
a momentary rorschach;
you are reassembled in the same second
25 million minutes away... face in the sand,
your ass mooning the sun

all alone in the long-dead timeline you sit
and face the sea

await the sirens. await the sky to shrink
and the screaming of teeth and hair follicles
to subsist into a collage of space and time
clinging to the tonsils of mathematics

but there is only the wind
and a seagull staring...

you smile and know yourself
to sit in complete safety for
the first time in all of time

but then: your serene is overtaken
by seven shadows / 7 exact other yous....
each scratching at napes and scalps,
shaking heads, sad as shit....

"it's happened again" 2 yous say

3 others, "i was gonna say that"

the remainders all laugh, knowingly.

same shirts. the same scars
from a bad day at preschool.

the same mustard stains
below the collar, 7 pockets
with $8 dollars.

and 43¢.

"the slave trade was massive. expansive
beyond our abilities to truly fathom.
more than some butterfly effect; for us
to trample time a stampede of whales
is needed, a Malcolm Xeroxed (if you will)

to the point of tipping; tripping Zeus."
the air before you burning
pinpricks of sun / the package of time
with its pickling heat / the atmosphere
pulsing and convulsing
as Chronos smacks his lips, opens
his throat to once again unswallow
Auset wanting her teat milk back

"here come another...." to the power of 4

"this could take some time" to the power of 2

"ah, you beat me to it" to the power of 3

"i have one: if a gathering of crows

is called a murder, what's a bundle of black
men who travel time to an ancient shore?"

a quintet shouts "a symphony of paradoxes!"

"AHA, NO! ...it's a leviathan of umbras...
but certainly yall knew that... right?"

the ninth steps out the void
tripping into paradise (a 27th by tomorrow)

"keep this up and we'll need a bigger abacus."

two days hence, the 44th, with ketchup
on a cuff and an ancient poem folded
in a pocket written, he'll say, in the future
in secret orbit of a martian moon / 8:43
tattooed below an ear:

"ode to the lineage of a single shadow
leviathians in slumber
within a gracious lap
in nap upon the labia
of a gracious ocean."

"at last, a trickle up!"

“the message is out!”

“alone we are a tribe.”

the seagull flies away

Protoplasmic Phrenology

I.

this pathos-by-proxy still twitches at the mere mention of paterollers storming the gate / neanderthals with knuckles dragging, swarming the stanza; dupes in white robes - haute-couture dunces capped in trivial pursuits; they've come for the gardenias, the organza. and the penumbra spills over every edge, haunted / no / daunted by a post-slavery stress disorder that's anything but paint-by-the-numbers. disembodied voices told me to buckle up / that work was to be done / that the dawn only came but once a day / "sumdirt, wake up."

but who knew i'd be the one to grow up mapping the spinal cortexes of Yoruba-Oblongata / talking the dead down from the ledges of ivory towers, stalking spirit-guides on chalkboards, in chat rooms, and in chapbooks (always in a state of rough-draft) that outline & underlay the pedagogy of a sun-people told for years how melanin was detrimental to accomplishment, undermining merit and our seats at the table; that it was in our DNA to be a recipient never the progenitor

winning bets were placed on the academic crowd-pleasers & social media favorites, but who thought it would come down to this: me: this son of a bitmap, this child of a low-down dirty diesel, this star-crossed witness taking the sacred stand on behalf of Stolen Property's™ refurbished indigenous literature: "yes, if it pleases the court; the accused was with me last night. we shared a bed. we shared a few words. and yes it's true, that during day - we're seldom seen together, but on my secret facebook account i kept photos...."

somewhere, a lot of kwacha just changed hands.

2.

the story goes I was born the son of an egun-runner and fell shadow-first from several wombs all at once; assembled on a single line and stitched into Eshu's saliva by the gnarled, ensorcelled hands of an unseen seamstress, but I digress. this poem is my mess-of-pieces and in haste I assumed you already knew the scientific weight of Sankofa and the configuration of electrons within a 'nations sack. you see, the double helix of most nursery rhymes are made of fairy atoms and colonial angst, but mine are composed of the Splinters from an Ancestral Poro Mask, Robert Johnson's Terrestrial Cigarette Ash, the Shards of Sun Ra's Celestial Birth Certificate, plus the Narrational Typing Ribbons from Things Fall Apart / Mumbo Jumbo / Good Times, Etc., etc. & the banana in the pocket of this poem is a poltergeist. but i'm no ghostbuster whispering the echos of the dead - i'm the doorman for the dearly dormant. it's a tough trade & not as in demand as you would think.

I was born to translate Tarbaby's Morse Code into a canonical course (jes grew 101), my dissertation was on head-lump reading. Baron Saturday was my first instructor. he paid me to re-edit the wikipage for the pot-liquor sciences and, like good credit, he taught me to be everywhere you want to be. that's why i'm known as Prometheus Backwash on twitter and, by luck of the drawl, i'm Juju-Chagalia on instagram. i'm told that upfromsumdirt is kiswahili for renaissance (i'm sure that's bullshit) & that my signature looks like Jean Michel's long lost rorschach, my John Hancock the sonogram for a dismantled subculture, you should see my cat-scan; no shit, my medulla is a fun-house mirror from hell.

I see Saint Octavia's silhouette weeping on toast, I see her cameo in the moles that I trace, like cosmic braille, between the breasts of my afroriginal lover - she too has a third eye, but her middle titty is a tunnel of light. you see, I was struck by a marching band as a baby and that's why I see everything so clearly. just didn't know that i'd be the one to grow up re-inventing a wonderland, replacing my over-imagined idea of good ol'

Rwanda for Kentucky as Uncle Tom's backdrop where cabins are shingled in soapstone and cowries with wallpapers written in sanskrit sampling the Jameses (the Brown one and the Baldwin one)... does anyone know the literary trajectory for an African American writer profiling himself? then again, it's not like I was born for recognition, having my mug on mugs, having "viva sumdirt!" silkscreened on t-shirts in every coffee house on an HBCU campus; brothadirt: the lone dissociative black poet always looking in at the MFA chitlin circuit after-party at AWP. god's honest truth, the tradition for upholding a metered, time-honored dialog is just not in me. I was born an act of reclamation. what need I with discursive progressions if the thought-process is afraid of flames? I shit fire; never learned to spit it or to hone it. and I can't really say, at this point, that I condone it. I never learned to 'career'... once I've opened my mouth I only careen. and according to the Academes, the windows of my soul are amateurishly viscid.

3.

as for you: continue taming your lions & chasing your gazelles while I suckle the breast-milk from the teats of hyenas (and other rescue animals); cream from the camel of a Midway, Kentucky farm dilutes my evening coffee: *what else am I to do?* I'm voodoo distilled in bourbon.

you see, it's in my nature to alert you to aneurysm; like a service dog, when I curl up at your feet it means a conniption or a hurricane or long-playing parable is coming. O' what a prescriptive medication this sloe discussion; I'm a long-lost son of Esu (or at least of Shaft) tipping through the elephant graveyard in ruby slippers, every poem louder than a balm, my hoodie more a cloak & cowl. or a caul. but decidedly not the threat you're told to think.

"Help Me Get The Body In The Trunk", "Dirt Farmer", "Caul & Response", "Black Begonias", and "Jean Rabin Gives Africa The Bird" appear in the printed collection, *Caul & Response* (Argus House/Winged City Press, 2015); "Popular Poem w/ Sharp Title", "Bus Fare For A Valkyrie", "In Deifying A Total Darkness", "Meth Lab At The Lollipop Guild", "Photographer Catches The Exact Moment A Volcano Erupts", "Bysshe, Please" (as "Prometheus Backwash"), "Modern Xenomorph", and "Protoplasmic Phrenology" appear in the chapbook *Chiaroscuro Vitae* (Radical Paper Press, 2019); "A Time Unraveller's Travel Journal" and "The Sankofa Paradox" appear in *The Time Unraveller's Travel Journal & Sankofa Paradox* (Radical Paper Press, 2019); "Crissy, From the Creek" and "Here, the Earth Giant Lays His Gentle Head" appear in *Anthology of Appalachian Writers Volume XII 2020*.

Releasing soon, *To Emit Teal* (poetry, Broadstone Books, fall 2020).

upfromsumdirt.com
ufsd@upfromsumdirt.com
gumroad.com/upfromsumdirt

Deifying A Total Darkness, poetry
copyright © upfromsumdirt, 2020
ISBN 978-1-934639-29-0

FIRST PRINT

art work & layout design by upfromsumdirt.
this book uses IM FELL DW Pica & Kingthings Exeter

shop local & support independent booksellers whenever possible

Harry Tankoos Books
Michael Scharf, editor
harrytankoos.cloud